D1524591

MILITARY COURTS

BARBARA M. LINDE

PowerKiDS
press™

NEW YORK

Published in 2020 by The Rosen Publishing Group, Inc.
29 East 21st Street, New York, NY 10010

Editor: Jane Katirgis
Book Design: Rachel Rising

Photo Credits: Cover Andrey_Popov/Shutterstock.com; Cover, pp.1, 3, 4, 5, 6, 7, 8, 9, 10, 11, 12, 13, 14, 15, 16, 17, 18, 19, 20, 21, 22, 23, 24, 25, 26, 27, 28, 29, 30, 31, 32 (background) Allgusak/Shutterstock.com; pp. 4, 12, 16, 26, 28, (gavel) AVA Bitter/Shutterstock.com; p. 5 Rena Schild/Shutterstock.com; p. 7 https://commons.wikimedia.org/wiki/File:Evacuation_Day_and_Washington%27s_Triumphal_Entry.jpg; p. 9 Courtesy of The Library of Congress; pp. 9, 17 (wood background) arigato/Shutterstock.com; p .10 vchal/Shutterstock.com; p. 11 Photographee.eu/Shutterstock.com; p. 13 https://commons.wikimedia.org/wiki/File:VADM_Nanette_M._DeRenzi.jpg; p. 14 https://commons.wikimedia.org/wiki/File:US_Navy_111219-N-ZZ999-076_A_visit,_board,_search_and_seizure_team_from_the_guided-missile_destroyer_USS_Pinckney_(DDG_91)_approaches_a_suspected_p.jpg; p. 15 https://commons.wikimedia.org/wiki/File:Somalian_Piracy_Threat_Map_2010.png; p. 17 https://jsc.defense.gov/Portals/99/Documents/MCM2016.pdf?ver=2016-12-08-181411-957; pp. 19, 21 Courtesy of U.S. Air Force; p. 23 Courtesy of U.S Navy; p. 25 Win McNamee/Getty Images News/Getty Images; p. 27 Stock Montage/Archive Photos/Getty Images; p. 29 https://commons.wikimedia.org/wiki/File:Billy_Mitchell_at_his_court-martial.jpg; p. 30 Madlen/Shutterstock.com.

Library of Congress Cataloging-in-Publication Data

Names: Linde, Barbara M., author.
Title: Military courts / Barbara M. Linde.
Description: New York : PowerKids Press, 2020. | Series: Court is in session
   | Includes index.
Identifiers: LCCN 2018027772| ISBN 9781538343265 (library bound) | ISBN
   9781538343241 (pbk.) | ISBN 9781538343258 (6 pack)
Subjects: LCSH: Courts-martial and courts of inquiry--United States--Juvenile
   literature. | Military offenses--United States--Juvenile literature. |
   Military law--United States--Juvenile literature. | Military
   discipline--United States--Juvenile literature.
Classification: LCC KF7620 .L56 2019 | DDC 343.73/0143--dc23
LC record available at https://lccn.loc.gov/2018027772

Manufactured in the United States of America

CPSIA Compliance Information: Batch #CSPK19. For further information contact Rosen Publishing, New York, New York at 1-800-237-9932.

Contents

THE U.S. ARMED FORCES 4

EARLY MILITARY JUSTICE 6

MODERN MILITARY JUSTICE 8

CRIMES COVERED 10

JUDGE ADVOCATE GENERAL CORPS 12

PROTECTION FROM PIRATES 14

THE COURT-MARTIAL PROCESS 16

LEVELS OF COURT-MARTIAL 18

THE SPECIAL COURT-MARTIAL 20

THE GENERAL COURT-MARTIAL 22

APPEALING A DECISION 24

THE COURT-MARTIAL OF BENEDICT ARNOLD 26

OTHER HISTORIC COURTS-MARTIAL 28

JUSTICE FOR ALL 30

GLOSSARY 31

INDEX 32

WEBSITES 32

THE U.S. ARMED FORCES

There are five branches of the U.S. armed forces with more than 2 million members among them. The U.S. Army is the main fighting force on land. The U.S. Navy's primary focus is the sea, while the U.S. Air Force focuses on the skies. The Marine Corps is a quick-response force that fights on land and sea. The U.S. Coast Guard keeps the waterways in and around the country safe.

Reserve Forces and the National Guard

Reserve forces are made up of people who complete some military training, continue occasional training, and stand by to help the full-time military in times of war or other trouble. In the United States, each military branch has its own reserve force. The United States also has the Air National Guard and the Army National Guard, which are similar but organized by state.

On June 6, 2014, a service member from each of the five branches of the military attended the 70th anniversary of D-Day in Washington, D.C.

COAST GUARD **AIR FORCE** **NAVY** **MARINE CORPS** **ARMY**

At times, members of the armed forces may be accused of committing crimes. In some of these cases, military members are subject to the military justice system and its laws. No matter where in the world they serve, these laws apply to all active members.

5

EARLY MILITARY JUSTICE

The first military justice system used in the United States was older than the country. It dated back to 1775, when the 13 British colonies in eastern North America raised an army and went to war with the British. The Continental Congress created the American Articles of War for the army and the Articles for the Government of the Navy for the colonies' ships. This system of rules, also known as codes, explained proper military behavior. The codes also listed the punishments for breaking military rules.

The colonies won their independence and formed the United States of America. In time, the country's leaders wrote the U.S. Constitution, which says that Congress can make rules to govern the military. The Constitution made the president the commander in chief of the armed forces.

This painting, titled "*Evacuation Day*" and Washington's Triumphal Entry in New York City, depicts General George Washington leading the Continental Army into New York City on November 25, 1783, after British troops were forced out.

MODERN MILITARY JUSTICE

These codes stayed in use, mostly unchanged, for many years. However, different branches of the military didn't always apply the rules the same way, and some members thought this was unfair. By 1941, many Americans began joining the military to fight in World War II. They were stationed all over the world. During the war, there were more than 2 million cases of American military members tried for breaking laws. Many people were unhappy with how the military handled this and the lack of rights for military members.

Starting in 1948, a committee created a new system of laws for the military services, called the Uniform Code of Military Justice (UCMJ). Congress approved the code, and all branches of the U.S. armed forces began using it in 1950.

FAST FACTS

Two committees meet every year to suggest changes and updates to the UCMJ. In 2016, stealing accomplished with credit and debit cards was added as an offense.

The UCMJ is meant to make sure all members of the military, anywhere in the world, are treated fairly if they are accused of wrongdoing.

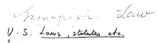

monograph Law
U.S. Laws, statutes, etc.

4 | 8
Com. | 1
| 4C

UNIFORM CODE
of
MILITARY JUSTICE

**Text, References and Commentary
based on the Report of the
Committee on a Uniform Code of
Military Justice to
The Secretary of Defense**
1949

/   2.11

MEMBERS OF
THE COMMITTEE ON A UNIFORM CODE OF MILITARY JUSTICE
AND ITS STAFF

COMMITTEE ON A UNIFORM CODE OF MILITARY JUSTICE

    Professor Edmund M. Morgan, Jr.
    Chairman
       (Professor of Law
        Harvard University)

    Honorable Gordon Gray
    Department of the Army Member
       (Assistant Secretary of the Army)

    Honorable W. John Kenney
    Department of the Navy Member
       (Under Secretary of the Navy)

    Honorable Eugene M. Zuckert
    Department of the Air Force Member
       (Assistant Secretary of the Air Force)

    Mr. Felix E. Larkin
    Executive Secretary
       (Assistant General Counsel
        Office of the Secretary of Defense)

WORKING GROUP

    Mr. Felix E. Larkin
    Chairman
       (Assistant General Counsel
        Office of the Secretary of Defense)

    Colonel John P. Dinsmore
    Department of the Army Representative
       (Legislative and Liaison Division
        Department of the Army)

    Lieutenant Colonel John M. Pitzer
    Department of the Army Representative
       (Office of the Judge Advocate General
        Department of the Army)

CRIMES COVERED

Some actions, such as stealing, drunk driving, and murder, are crimes under both military and **civilian** law. However, if members of the military commit these offenses, they go through the military courts for trial and punishment.

A police officer tests a driver's alcohol level. Drunk driving is a military and a civilian crime.

Other actions are considered crimes in the military, but not in civilian life. These affect good order and **discipline** in the military. Desertion, or abandoning the military, and being absent without leave, or permission, are two such actions. Disobeying orders and disrespect of superiors are also covered. The UCMJ includes punishments for military members who misbehave in front of an enemy, help the enemy, or act as spies.

JUDGE ADVOCATE GENERAL CORPS

The U.S. Army, Navy, Air Force, and Marine Corps each have a legal branch called the Judge **Advocate** General's (JAG) Corps. A judge advocate general leads each branch. A judge advocate is a full-time officer in the military and a trained attorney, or lawyer. Military judges also come from the JAG Corps. Members of the JAG Corps are stationed all over the world. The Navy JAG Corps has members on most ships and on bases.

The Judge Advocate General

A judge advocate general is a high-ranking military officer. For a long time, only men held these positions. Vice Admiral Nanette DeRenzi became the first female judge advocate general for the U.S. Navy in 2012. Brigadier General Flora D. Darpino became the first female U.S. Army judge advocate general in 2013.

Vice Admiral Nanette DeRenzi became the first female judge advocate general for the U.S. Navy in 2012.

Judge advocates assist members of the military with many things, including legal help with car accidents, wills, divorces, home purchases, or contracts. They also serve as **prosecutors** if someone is accused of a crime. Commanders often use judge advocates to help them make sure they're following military rules and United States laws correctly.

PROTECTION FROM PIRATES

Pirates are still a very real threat to military and civilian ships. The United States Navy works with other countries and businesses to find ways to defeat pirates. When doing so, U.S. Navy judge advocates make sure the international laws about fighting on the seas are followed. This is important so that the military forces of the different countries can work well together. Also, when pirates are captured, they can be brought to trial and the trials can go forward.

FAST FACTS

The main areas for piracy are off the Horn of Africa, in the Gulf of Guinea, and in the waters around Southeast Asia.

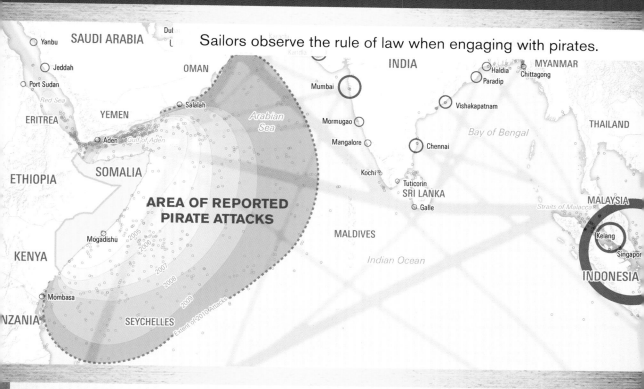

Sailors observe the rule of law when engaging with pirates.

In 2010, sailors captured six Somali pirates when they tried to take over the USS *Ashland* in the Gulf of Aden. The men were brought to trial in Norfolk, Virginia. All of them were sentenced to time in jail, with one pirate getting a life sentence.

THE COURT-MARTIAL PROCESS

If a member of the military is accused of committing an offense, the member's commanding officer will follow the rules in the *Manual for Courts-Martial*, which is part of the UCMJ. First, the commanding officer will look into the matter. Depending on the results, they may do nothing, issue a nonjudicial punishment, or start one of three levels of the formal court-martial process. This is called "preferring" charges.

Article 15

An Article 15, which is otherwise known as a nonjudicial punishment, is the most common type of military discipline. It doesn't need a full trial and doesn't cause a criminal record. In fact, sometimes it's completely removed from military records. This type of discipline is usually for minor problems, such as being late for duty or sleeping on watch. Punishments may include losing some pay or extra duties.

Every military trial follows the rules in the *Manual for Courts-Martial United States.*

PREFACE

The Manual for Courts-Martial (MCM), United States (2016 Edition) updates the MCM (2012 Edition). It is a complete reprinting and incorporates the MCM (2012 Edition), including all amendments to the Preamble, Rules for Courts-Martial (R.C.M.), Military Rules of Evidence (Mil. R. Evid.), Punitive Articles, and Nonjudicial Punishment Procedures made by the President in Executive Orders (EO) from 1984 to present, and specifically including EO 13643 (15 May 2013); EO 13669 (13 June 2014); EO 13696 (17 June 2015); EO 13730 (20 May 2016); and EO 13740 (16 September 2016). *See* Appendix 25. This edition also contains amendments to the Uniform Code of Military Justice (UCMJ) made by the National Defense Authorization Acts (NDAA) for Fiscal Years 2014 through 2016. Finally, this edition incorporates amendments to the Supplementary Materials accompanying the MCM as published in the Federal Register on 8 July 2015, 16 July 2015, 22 March 2016, 15 June 2016, 8 November 2016, and 8 December 2016. The aforementioned NDAAs, EOs, and Supplementary Materials are available at the Joint Service Committee on Military Justice website at http://jsc.defense.gov. Because this manual includes numerous changes, practitioners should consider the MCM completely revised.

JOINT SERVICE COMMITTEE ON MILITARY JUSTICE

A court-martial is the military version of a trial. At this time, the accused person may get a judge advocate to help with their defense. They can also hire a civilian lawyer.

LEVELS OF COURT-MARTIAL

There are three levels of court-martial: **summary**, special, and general. The type used depends on how serious the crime is and if the person is **enlisted** or an officer.

A summary court-martial is only for enlisted members and only for less serious offenses, such as disrespect or being absent without leave. It's much like a nonjudicial punishment. An officer who's in the same branch of the military as the accused hears the case. Before the hearing, the accused may talk with a judge advocate for free and may also pay for a civilian lawyer. If the accused is found guilty, punishments might include being moved to a lower rank, losing part of one's pay for one or two months, or not being allowed to leave the base or ship.

FAST FACTS

Many United States military bases around the world have courtrooms where a court-martial can be held. If a regular courtroom is not available, a temporary courtroom can be set up in any building or even in a tent. For the U.S. Navy, a court-martial can be held on a ship.

An airman (standing, right) who's an assistant staff judge advocate asks a question during a mock trial for Air Force airmen.

THE SPECIAL COURT-MARTIAL

Special courts-martial can apply to both enlisted members and officers. They're usually for middle-level offenses. A judge advocate defends the accused, or defendant, and another judge advocate prosecutes the defendant for the military. The accused may have a judge hear the case with or without a jury made up of at least three military members, or they may ask for only the jury to hear the case. If the defendant is found guilty, the sentence may include **confinement**, loss of pay, or a bad conduct **discharge**.

In one recent case, an Air Force airman was found guilty of **dereliction** of duty, using illegal drugs, and being absent without leave. She was confined for 60 days, lost over $3,000 in pay, and got a bad conduct discharge.

There are five kinds of discharges. A bad conduct discharge is given only to enlisted members. It's used for less serious crimes.

Captain Brian Adams talks to airmen during a mock trial.

21

THE GENERAL COURT-MARTIAL

General courts-martial can be used for any crime under the UCMJ, but they're usually used for the most serious offenses. These may include war crimes such as hurting or killing an enemy civilian or military member. The jury has at least five members; an enlisted person may ask that one-third of the jurors also be enlisted. If the death penalty is a possible punishment, there must be a jury, so the accused can't ask for a trial by the judge only.

In 2018, a Marine who broke into a house and stole military and personal property underwent a general court-martial and was sentenced to 18 months in prison, fined $11,500, lowered in rank, and given a bad conduct discharge.

FAST FACTS

A dishonorable discharge can only be given after an enlisted member is found guilty though a general court-martial. The term for the same thing for an officer is a **"dismissal."** Someone who receives either one might have trouble finding work after leaving the military.

Vice Admiral James Crawford III, judge advocate general, discusses a case with legal experts.

APPEALING A DECISION

All court-martial convictions go through an appeal, when a "**convening** authority" looks at the case again. This is the officer who made the arrangements for the court-martial. This person can agree with the sentence, reduce it, or dismiss the case. Any punishment of a discharge, more than a year in prison, or the death penalty goes to the military branch's Court of Criminal Appeals. Three military judges look over the case to make sure the laws have been correctly followed. The panel may reduce the sentence, dismiss the charges, or order a new trial.

The U.S. Court of Appeals for the Armed Forces reviews cases that have a death penalty sentence and other cases that the JAG Corps sends it. This court has civilian, not military, judges.

The appeals process makes sure all rules and regulations have been followed, and that all defendants get a fair trial.

THE COURT-MARTIAL OF BENEDICT ARNOLD

Major General Benedict Arnold started out as a Revolutionary War hero, but in 1779, he had one of the first courts-martial in the new United States of America. In 1778, Arnold was the military governor of Philadelphia when Joseph Reed, a politician, made several charges against him. Arnold said he was innocent and that Reed made up the charges.

In Arnold's Own Words

Benedict Arnold wrote these words to the court near the end of his court-martial:

> "I have looked forward with pleasing anxiety [desire] to the present day, when, by the judgment of my fellow soldiers, I shall (I doubt not) stand honorable acquitted [found not guilty] of all the charges brought against me, and again share with them the glory and danger of this just war."

Arnold wasn't quite correct, as he was found guilty of some of the charges.

Not long after his court-martial, Arnold became a traitor when he sold secrets to the British army.

The court found Arnold guilty of letting a ship leave the closed port of Philadelphia and of using public wagons to move personal goods. (Arnold said he paid to use the wagons.) He was found not guilty of the other charges. The court ordered General George Washington to scold Arnold in a published letter. Arnold was angry with Washington; he didn't think he deserved the public **reprimand**.

OTHER HISTORIC COURTS-MARTIAL

In 1867, Civil War hero and Army officer George Armstrong Custer was charged with 11 offenses, including misconduct and leaving his post in Kansas without approval. Custer pled not guilty. He was found guilty of five of the charges. He lost his rank and pay for one year. After that, he went back on active duty.

"The Father of the Air Force"

After he resigned from the U.S. Army, William Mitchell kept insisting that the U.S. Air Force should be separate from the Army. He wrote articles and talked with members of Congress, military leaders, and the general public. He became known as "the Father of the Air Force" after the Department of the Air Force was created in 1947. An aircraft bomber (the B-25 Mitchell) and General Mitchell International Airport in Milwaukee, Wisconsin, are both named for him.

Colonel Billy Mitchell stands at his court-martial.

Colonel William "Billy" Mitchell was an Army pilot who strongly believed in the use of military aircraft. In 1925, he publicly blamed several aircraft accidents on poor leadership at the highest levels of the U.S. Navy and War Departments. He was found guilty of **insubordination**. Instead of accepting the punishment (loss of rank and half pay for five years), Mitchell left the U.S. Army.

JUSTICE FOR ALL

For many years, members of the colonial and United States military have bravely defended the colonies and then the new nation. The Continental Congress saw the need for a military justice system, and the early leaders of the United States of America improved on it. Later, government leaders once again made necessary changes and created the Uniform Code of Military Justice.

The UCMJ has served the U.S. armed forces well for almost 70 years. Enlisted members and officers in the U.S. Army, Air Force, Marine Corps, Navy, and Coast Guard are guaranteed equal and fair treatment whenever the need arises. The military court system of the United States is meant to protect the rights of members of the armed forces, as they protect the United States itself.

GLOSSARY

advocate: A person who argues for or supports a cause, person, or policy.

civilian: A person not on active duty in the military.

confinement: The state of being confined, or limited to a certain location.

convene: To come together to meet.

dereliction: Neglecting something on purpose.

discharge: Separation from military service.

discipline: To control by enforcing obedience or order.

dismissal: The act of dismissing, or removing from position or service.

enlisted: Members of the military who rank below a certain level of officers.

insubordination: Being disobedient to authority.

prosecutor: A lawyer who prosecutes, or argues charges against, an accused person in court.

reprimand: A severe or official scolding.

summary: Done without delay or formality.

INDEX

A

Air Force, U.S., 4, 5, 12, 19, 20, 28, 30
Air National Guard, 4
American Articles of War, 6
Army, U.S., 4, 5, 12, 28, 29, 30
Army National Guard, 4
Arnold, Benedict, 26, 27
Articles for the Government of the Navy, 6

C

Coast Guard, U.S., 4, 5, 30
Congress, U.S., 6, 8, 28
Constitution, U.S., 6
Continental Congress, 6, 30
court-martial, 16, 17, 18, 19, 20, 22, 23, 24, 26, 28, 29
Court of Appeals for the Armed Forces, U.S., 24
Court of Criminal Appeals, 24
Custer, George Armstrong, 28

D

Darpino, Flora D., 12, 13
DeRenzi, Nanette, 12, 13
discharge, 20, 21, 22, 23, 24

J

judge advocate, 12, 13, 14, 17, 18, 19, 20, 23

Judge Advocate General's (JAG) Corps, 12, 24

M

Manual for Courts-Martial, 16, 17
Marine Corps, 4, 5, 12, 22, 30
Mitchell, William, 28, 29

N

Navy, U.S., 4, 5, 12, 13, 14, 19, 29, 30
nonjudicial punishment, 16, 18

U

Uniform Code of Military Justice (UCMJ), 8, 9, 11, 16, 22, 30

WEBSITES

Due to the changing nature of Internet links, PowerKids Press has developed an online list of websites related to the subject of this book. This site is updated regularly. Please use this link to access the list: www.powerkidslinks.com/courts/military